妥

妥

I

Scream

Koans

The Secret Zen Wisdom of Children's Literature

by

Brian Rock

妥

妥

"Let us feed on joy"

\- Buddha

Copyright 2018 Brian Rock

Published by First Light Publishing
Richmond, VA

Library of Congress Control Number: 2018948047

Rock, Brian. I Scream Koans
The Secret Zen Wisdom of Children's Literature

Summary: Meditations on spiritual truths contained in classic
and contemporary children's literature.

ISBN# 978-0-9754411-6-9

1. Religion. 2. Spirituality. 3. Buddhism. 4. Christianity.
5. Children's Literature

Introduction

A koan is a traditional Zen Buddhist technique to stimulate awareness beyond thinking. (Zen, by the way, simply means "meditation.")

The most famous example is, "What is the sound of one hand clapping?"

Your first instinct is to think it doesn't make a sound at all. But what if silence is the answer? How do we still our mind to achieve that level of silence? But clapping is a way of getting attention or showing approval. So, what is the one had clapping for? Are we trying to get our own attention? And on and on the questions pile up.

So, you see, the koan is designed to be a paradox, a riddle without an answer. It is designed to point out the limits of logical thinking, and thereby lead to enlightenment.

The word koan actually means "legal case" or "file of legal documents." In the rigid, bureaucratic hierarchy of ancient China, many court cases were literally matters of life or death.

妥

妥

Zen masters chose the term to emphasize the importance of attaining enlightenment – you are either spiritually alive or you are spiritually dead. Although the truth contained in each koan is serious, the koan itself, or the key to unlocking the koan may appear comical, nonsensical, even childish. Yet another paradox on the path to enlightenment.

And, of course, enlightenment is not limited to any one era of time, or place, or culture. Zen Buddhism itself evolved over time with input from India, China, Japan, and Southeast Asia. And as the writings of Thich Nhat Hanh and Marcus Borg illustrate, Siddhartha Gautama (aka The Buddha) would have recognized Jesus Christ as a fellow Zen master. There are modern commentators who regard baseball legend Yogi Berra, and other non-Buddhists as modern-day Zen masters as well. (For those interested in learning more about the history of Zen and Koans, I have included a brief reading list at the end of this book.)

With this in mind, I incorporate both Eastern and Western spiritual terminology (and historical figures) throughout this book to accommodate readers from different traditions. As The Tibetan Book of Living and Dying by Sogyal Rinpoche notes, "Saints and mystics throughout history have adorned their realizations with different names... but what they are all fundamentally experiencing is the essential nature of the mind. Christians and Jews call it "God"; Hindus call it... "Brahman," Sufi mystics name it "the Hidden Essence," and Buddhists call it "buddha nature."

I use the word, "God" in place of the "buddha nature," as most Western readers are more familiar with this term. Please feel free to mentally substitute whatever terms work best for you where appropriate.

The point is, for the truly aware, a moment of Zen can be found anywhere; and an enlightenment-inspiring koan can come from anyplace; even the pages of a children's book.

Which leads us to...

妥

妥

"Did you ever

stop

to

think,

and forget to start again?"

A.A. Milne

Winnie The Pooh

Sometimes we get so caught up in thinking, plotting, and planning, that we forget to act. Sometimes we get so caught up in working, exercising, and just getting through the day, that we forget to think.

But thinking without acting is pointless

And acting without thinking is reckless

Here lies the very heart of Zen: the balancing of opposites. The path to enlightenment requires harmony between the competing impulses of human nature - Masculine/Feminine, Active/Receptive, Mental/Emotional, etc.

But to bring ourselves into balance requires an awareness of our own imbalance. So take a moment, two or three times a day to just BE AWARE. Or in the words of Zen Master Ikkyu, "Attention! Attention! Attention!" Ask yourself if you're thinking too much and doing too little; or giving too much and not allowing yourself to receive. Then make an effort to do or be more of what you lack.

And if it feels awkward at first, don't worry. If a "bear of very little brain" can do it, so can you!

妥

妥

"Harold knew that the

HIGHER

up he went,
The farther he could see."

Crocket Johnson

Harold & The Purple Crayon

☯

Harold takes his purple crayon, creates a new world, and then steps into it.

So do we all.

Whether we know it or not, we create our own reality, our own ups and downs, and our own destiny.

In the words of the Buddha, "Whatever a monk pursues with his thinking and pondering, that becomes the inclination of his awareness." Or as it is often paraphrased, "What you think, you become."

If we choose to wallow in the depths of fear and self-pity, then the reality we create is very dark and dense. Which in turn makes it hard to see the beauty that surrounds us.

But if we choose to rise to our highest ideals of love and hope and charity; then we create a light and luminous reality. We become better able to see the good in others and ourselves.

With enough practice, we might even join the Masters and Saints (and Harold himself) and be able to see far enough to find our way home to our original, radiant (and possibly purple) Spirit Self.

妥

妥

"No act of kindness,
no matter how
small,
is ever wasted."

Aesop

Aesop's Fables

The law of Karma states that what you do to others will one day be done to you.

Most people understand this as a form of delayed punishment. If you steal from your neighbor, one day someone will steal from you.

But there is also a positive side to Karma. The acts of kindness you do to others also return to you. As Buddha put it, "If you do not tend one another, then who is there to tend you?"

And beyond the karmic balance sheet, there is a deeper understanding. Just as Jesus said, "Whatsoever you do to the least of these, you do unto me;" your every interaction with a living being is an interaction with the Divine. For the Divine Spirit lives in us all. And your acts of kindness are nothing less than gifts to God.

妥

妥

"When you are

REAL

shabbiness doesn't matter."

Margery Williams

The Velveteen Rabbit

☯

Appearances can be deceiving.

A shiny, new car can break down on the highway. A fancy toy with whistles and lights can be rather boring. A smiling face can hide a devious mind.

Likewise, a rusty car may have a precision engine. A tattered toy may give years of enjoyment. And a haggard face may cover a beautiful soul.

In the end, appearances always give way to the truth. Or in the words of the Buddha, "Three things shine before the world and cannot be hidden: the moon, the sun, and the truth."

Whoever says, "Clothes make the man," has never spent any time developing their mind or heart or soul. And those are the places we should look first to assess someone's character. Again, the Buddha tells us, "What good is hide clothing? While your inward state is a tangle, you polish your exterior."

How someone looks is irrelevant, and often misleading.

In this book about quotes from books, it is appropriate to remember to never judge a book by its cover.

妥

妥

"I like it better here where I can just sit quietly and smell the

flowers."

Munro Leaf
The Story of Ferdinand

In the pastures where young Ferdinand is raised, other bulls snort and charge and butt heads. They strive to impress each other and the watching cows and the visiting bull fight promoters.

But Ferdinand just sits and smells the flowers.

Like the other bulls in this story, many of us want to earn the respect of our friends, the love of another, or the right to be promoted.

But Ferdinand just sits and smells the flowers.

Like the other bulls, we are locked in a constant struggle to prove ourselves. Our respect waxes and wanes with our strength. Our love is bought in exchange for our accomplishments. And the glory of our success fades with the next person's success. And in the end, we struggle in vain as the beauty of life passes us by.

But Ferdinand just sits and smells the flowers.

Like the Buddha, he understands that, "with the relinquishing of all thought and egotism, the enlightened one is liberated through not clinging."

And as the world strives around him, Ferdinand is at peace as he sits and smells the flowers.

妥

妥

"It's fun to feel

isn't it?"

Dav Pilkey

Captain Underpants and the
Revolting Revenge of the
Radioactive Robo-Boxers

It *is* fun to feel offended. When someone says or does something that offends us, we feel so... superior. And that makes us feel good about ourselves, without actually having to do anything.

"I'm offended that you don't act like me."

"I'm offended that you don't think like me."

"I'm offended that you're not offended at the thing I'm offended at!"

These are just different ways of saying, "I'm better than you." Being offended is your ego tricking you into thinking you're more important than someone else.

We are all equal in the eyes of God. We're all trying to find our way. And we *all* make mistakes along the way.

As the Buddha says, "The faults of others are easier to see than one's own." But that doesn't mean we aren't without our own faults.

So, if you disagree with someone, try to feel some compassion for them. Try to remember your own faults. Try to find the common humanity between you.

Then, and only then, can you move toward reconciliation. And that is even more fun than being offended.

妥

妥

"If you ever find yourself in the

wrong story,

leave."

Mo Willems

Goldilocks & The
Three Dinosaurs

☯

So often we find ourselves in circumstances that are not to our liking.

"I hate my job."

"My boyfriend doesn't listen to me."

"That big lizard ate my donut!"

But if we stop to analyze the situation, we will realize that we have created our own situations.

Maybe we should have studied more in school.

Maybe we should spend as much time listening to others as we do talking to them.

Maybe we shouldn't carry sugary sweets into the reptile room of the zoo.

But the good news is, since we created our unpleasant conditions, we can also create pleasant conditions as well.

And as Udamavarga observed, "He who has done what is right is free from fear."

Think about the outcome you want. Imagine what it feels like to be there. Then Do The Right Thing to step into the story you want to live.

妥

妥

"Grown-ups never understand anything by themselves, and it is TIRESOME for children to be always and forever explaining things to them."

Antoine de Saint-Exupery

The Little Prince

Robert Fulgham famously wrote, "Everything I need to know, I learned in kindergarten."

And there is great truth to that.

Take turns. Share. Wash your hands. Don't eat stuff off the sidewalk.

Those are all valuable lessons, and still relevant after all these years.

But the most important thing that kids know, is how to see the world with eyes of wonder.

To a child, a quartz geode is a treasure. It's hidden in the earth. It has beautiful color. It sparkles in the sunlight.

But to an adult, it's just a piece of rock.

A diamond, on the other hand, will cause adults to pay large sums of money or even cheat or steal to obtain it.

Why? Because it's hidden in the earth, it has beautiful color, and it sparkles in the sunlight?

No. Because someone else tells them it's worth a lot of money.

So adults become cynics who know the cost of everything but the value of nothing.

And children must forever remind them to stop and enjoy the sunset or the passing ducklings or a simple moment snuggled on the couch.

妥

妥

"It brings such joy and

HappineSS;

I don't see many frowns.

But, just like any other job,

It has its **ups** and **downs**."

(from the poem, Jake the Yo-Yo Maker)

Kenn Nesbitt

The Biggest Burp Ever

There is a common misconception that enlightenment means no more struggle or effort.

But this traditional Zen koan proves otherwise:

> Before Enlightenment: chop wood, carry water,
> After Enlightenment: chop wood, carry water.

So being enlightened doesn't prevent struggle or effort. As long as you have a physical body, you are responsible for its maintenance.

However, being enlightened makes you better able to cope with the tasks of the physical world.

Finding enjoyment in those tasks is the key. If you love your job, you'll never really have to "work." Yes, there will be ups and downs, but enjoying the process makes them so much easier to handle.

And if you don't love your job? Begin the process to find a new one. Stop thinking in terms of paychecks and start thinking in terms of experiences that are meaningful to you. Then figure out how to get paid for doing them.

By the time we're ten most of us already know what we enjoy doing. Get back in touch with your inner ten year old and find a way to get paid for doing what you love!

And if you can't find a job right away – volunteer. Soon you'll build enough experience to find the job you love. And in the meantime you'll be nourishing your soul by doing what you love!

妥

妥

"Those who don't

believe

in magic will never find it."

Roald Dahl

The Minpins

Subatomic physicists don't know if light is a particle or a wave. It has properties of both.

The problem is, when they test light for particle traits, they can't detect the wave traits. And when they try to test for wave traits, they can no longer identify the particle traits.

In other words, they can only ever find what they *expect* to find with their tests.

So it is with life.

For every great invention, there were hundreds of people who said it couldn't be done. In 1900, most people didn't believe that human flight was possible. So most people didn't invent the airplane. And yet the airplane is with us today.

As Thich Nhat Hanh explains; "In the spring, you don't see any lemons on the tree, yet you know the lemons are there." Whether you believe or not, the lemons will appear. The only difference is, the believer will come back to harvest the fruit.

It only takes one person to believe in something to make it real. You may have to work at it, but you *can* make the impossible a reality.

Magic is real.

It lives in us all.

You just have to believe.

妥

妥

"Just because we don't **Understand** doesn't mean the explanation doesn't exist."

Madeline L'Engle

A Wrinkle in Time

It's funny that some people who think they are the smartest can be the most foolish. They reach the limits of their understanding and then they decree that nothing can exist beyond it. Like the Zen parable of pouring tea into a full cup, they are so filled with ego there is no room for anything else.

They say that God can't be observed in a laboratory, God can't be measured and quantified; therefore, God doesn't exist. But God cannot be contained in a beaker, yet there is nothing you can put in a beaker that doesn't contain God.

Leonardo da Vinci, Isaac Newton, Albert Einstein and all the scientific geniuses of the past understood that God was present in their science. And it was that understanding and faith that helped them move past the limits of their own knowing and shine new light into the unknown.

Only people who understand that they don't understand everything can continue to grow mentally and spiritually. Knowing our limitations is the first step to overcoming them, and therefore the first step to enlightenment.

You can not think your way to God. Bu there is another way of understanding. By opening your heart, you may discover secrets that are hidden from even the greatest of minds.

妥

妥

"'What's

miraculous

about a spider's web?'

said Mrs. Arable...

'Ever try to spin one?'

asked Dr. Dorian."

E.B. White

Charlotte's Web

There are those who say, "There's no such thing as miracles."

When miracles do occur, they call them 'mass psychosis' or 'spontaneous remissions' or 'anomalies.'

But labeling something isn't the same as understanding it. In fact, it quite often has the opposite effect. Once we place a label on something, we cease to look any further.

It's just a spider's web.

But of all the creatures on earth, only spiders make webs –why? How does the spider know to make the radial threads non-sticky and the circular threads sticky?

The fact that there is life at all is itself a miracle. And the unique expressions of life in millions of forms from insects to humans, to trees is also miraculous.

Jesus said in the Gospel of Thomas, "Split a piece of wood and I am there." By that He means that God is present in all things, even something as fleeting as a spider's web. Even in the spider that spun it. Even in the human who saw it. The miracle of Divine presence is all around; if you're willing to notice it.

妥

妥

"The world is so full of a number of things, I 'm sure we should all be as HAPPY AS KINGS."

Robert Louis Stevenson

A Child's Garden of Verses

We are indeed kings and queens. And our kingdoms are the sum of all the choices we've made in our lives. And yet, very few of us are "happy as kings."

We often feel like happiness is just out of reach. If only we had a better job, then we'd be happy. If only we had a spouse, or a nicer home, or…

And yet when we do get these things the newness wears off and we start the cycle again. If only I had…

But possessions, jobs, even relationships come and go. The only thing that is truly ours is our own soul. So be mindful of it. Be good to it. Take time to nourish your soul. Take time to notice the blessings in your kingdom.

And perhaps follow the advice of Fa-kheu-pi-a: "If only the thoughts be directed to that which is right, then happiness must necessarily follow."

When you stop worrying about the "next thing," and can be at peace with yourself; then you can begin to enjoy the many miracles of God's creation. And once you begin to notice these many blessings, you will be, "as happy as kings."

妥

妥

"I can't let safety and

security

become the focus of my
life."

Judy Blume

Tiger Eyes

If you ever go hang gliding, one of the first things your instructor will tell you is, "wherever you focus your eyes, that's where you will go."

The same is true of life.

If you only focus on safety and security, you may very well end up being safe. But at what cost?

Sitting on the couch is safer than exercising at the gym. But exercising will give you more energy and health. You may also make a new friend in the process.

Keeping a dead-end job is more secure than taking classes and applying for a new job. But landing a job that you enjoy will be more fulfilling.

Taken to the extreme, obsession with security can become its own prison. Which is why Buddha said, "May fear and dread not conquer me."

All the safety precautions in the world won't enable you to live forever. But if you never venture beyond your comfort zone, you will never have lived at all.

Break free of the chains of safety and security, and trust that God loves you and wants you to be happy. Let God be the wind beneath your wings as you glide into amazing new possibilities.

妥

妥

"You have striven with
all your

heart...

now you have risen to the
aerial world."

Hans Christian Anderson

The Little Mermaid

Spoiler Alert!

If you only know the Little Mermaid from Disney, you may want to read the original version before continuing…

In Hans Christian Anderson's original tale, the little mermaid dies. Consequently many people view this tale as a tragedy.

But they miss the point.

According to Anderson, mermaids are born without a soul and when they die, they dissolve into nothingness.

But because of her bravery and love, the mermaid in Anderson's story is able to win a soul before she dies. She is therefore able to live forever in heaven.

As Kshemendra notes, "Compassion alone sanctifies."

So we see that death is not the tragedy, it is a natural part of life's continuous cycle.

Living without loving and giving and striving for your soul's growth is the only real tragedy.

妥

妥

"I think I *can!*

I think I *can!*"

Watty Piper
The Little Engine That Could

I'm sure the little engine that could, like all of us, had friends or relatives that told her, "I think you CAN'T!"

So when she faced a challenge, she had to choose whether to believe the voices of those closest to her or her own inner voice.

And if she had heeded the voices of her (possibly well intentioned) friends, she never would have made it over the mountain. Even one moment of doubt could have stopped her in her tracks.

For doubt is the great enemy of achievement. It turns molehills into mountains and stops all forward progress.

Some of the greatest minds in the world will go unrecognized by history because they doubted their own abilities. Meanwhile, lesser lights will shine through the ages because they had the conviction to believe in themselves.

In truth, there is no limit to what the human mind can achieve - if it believes.

As Buddha said, "A monk who is skilled in concentration can cut the Himalayas in two."

Think about that!

妥

妥

"So many things are

POSSIBLE

just as long as you don't know they're

IMPOSSIBLE."

Norton Juster

The Phantom Tollbooth

"The earth is flat," "the sun revolves around the earth," "man was never meant to fly..."

It's funny how things we know for certain aren't always certain.

The science, it seems, is never completely settled.

What is impossible to today's science will be commonplace for tomorrow's.

Today we have cars that parallel park themselves, we have space probes landing on the surface of Mars, we have 3D printers that can create human organs. Who knows what impossible things we'll discover tomorrow!

As Nelson Mandela said, "It always seems impossible until it's done."

So, when you find yourself frustrated, or stuck or without hope; and when you've tried every possible thing you can think of to make things better, without success – start trying the impossible!

The only limit to what you can achieve is your own imagination!

妥

妥

"Don't go trying to use the same route twice. Indeed, don't try to get there at all. It'll happen when you're **not** looking for it."

C. S. Lewis

The Lion, The Witch, And The Wardrobe

We are all one.

We all come from the same Source. We all return to the same Source.

Like the Zen concept of the wave asking about the ocean, we are all nothing less than God expressing God's own Self through us.

This is the great secret to spiritual awareness and enlightenment, and the underlying truth of all true religions.

The only thing that makes us different is the infinite nature of God and our own free will.

So, the only difference between friends and enemies is that we see our best traits in our friends and our worst traits in our enemies.

Whether we know it or not, we are following the Buddha's directive to, "Consider others as yourself."

It follows then, that the more we cultivate our best qualities, the more we see others as friends. The more we cultivate our spirit nature, the more we recognize our kindred spirits – and there are indeed, so many of them!

妥

"I know who I **was** when I got up this morning, but I think I must have been

changed

several times since then."

Lewis Carroll
Alice's Adventures
in Wonderland

We play so many roles in life. We are children. We are parents. We are students. We are teachers. We are lovers. We are fighters…

Sometimes we play different roles in the same day.

We act one way around our parents. We act another way around our children. We speak more to those we're trying to teach. We listen more to those we're trying to learn from.

We change how we act and, essentially, who we are depending on with whom we interact.

But labels like parent, child, teacher, student are all illusions. We are all luminous, spirit beings. We are all equal in the sight of God, if we could just still our minds to perceive.

In the Zen koan, "Your mind moves," two monks argue over a flag. One says the flag is moving. The other says the wind is moving. A third monk passes by and says, "Not the wind, not the flag, mind is moving."

Don't be distracted by flags and labels. Still your mind and be true to your unchanging, inner Self.

妥

妥

"I wish to hatch my

own

eggs."

Beatrix Potter

The Tale of Jemima

Puddle-Duck

There is no substitute for experience.

If you wish to play piano, you could listen to the greatest piano concertos ever written. You could study the history of the piano. You could even attend a concert by a master virtuoso. But nothing short of putting your own fingers to the keyboard will enable you to learn how to play.

So it is with enlightenment. Reading the works of others and attending lectures is no substitute for daily, direct practice.

There is a story of a student who asked a monk, "What is the meaning of Zen?" The monk answered, "I'd like to tell you, but right now I have to go to the bathroom." The student looked puzzled, so the monk continued, "I know it's a trivial thing, but can you do it for me?"

Just as no one else can perform bodily functions for us, no one else can perform spiritual functions for us. It's up to all of us to, "hatch our own eggs!"

妥

妥

"Maybe we are all cabinets of Wonders!"

Brian Selznik
The Invention of
Hugo Cabret

Have you ever found some spare change under your sofa cushions? Have you ever come across a favorite article of clothing that you haven't worn in months? Have you ever found a cherished family heirloom tucked away in a forgotten corner?

We are surrounded by wonders and surprises. But all too often we fail to notice.

The same is true of ourselves.

We get so set in a routine that we develop blinders to anything outside of our repeated, daily actions. But that wasn't always the case.

There was a time when we soared with dragons, danced at royal balls and saved the planet. Like our forgotten family heirloom, those dreams are still within us.

As the Buddha said, "All that we are is the result of what we have thought."

So why not step outside of our routine and open some of the dustier cabinets of our memories. Who knows what wonders we'll find there!

妥

妥

"Like all magnificent
things, it's very
simple."

Natalie Babbitt
Tuck Everlasting

Sending a rocket to the moon is a magnificent feat of science. It involves thousands of precise calculations and years of equipment design. But at its core, it all comes down to achieving enough thrust.

Once scientists understand the simple foundational principal, they can build from there to achieve the magnificent.

But the most magnificent thing a human can achieve is union with God, or awakening the Divine within. There are many complex rituals and extensive scriptures that can guide one on the way. But once again, it helps to identify the simple foundational principle that underlies the complex equations.

According to the Buddha, the key to union with God and the universe (Nivrana) is contained in his third Noble Truth: Release all desire (Nirodha.)

Likewise, the simple foundation of Christianity is defined by Jesus as: Love God, love your neighbor, and love yourself.

Imagine a world where everyone loved their neighbor without any desire to be repaid in kind. Wouldn't that be magnificent?

妥

妥

"To have faith is to have
WINGS."

J. M. Barrie

Peter Pan

In the words of that Zen master Henry Ford, "Whether you think you can, or you think you can't – you're right."

Either way it comes down to faith. Before attempting something, you either have faith that you can do it, or you have faith that you can't.

If you have faith that you can't do something, your mind immediately saps the will and persistence needed to accomplish your task. It becomes a self-fulfilling prophecy.

But if you have faith that you CAN do something, your will, strength, focus and energy are all increased. Each setback is a certain indication that you are making progress. Each discouraging comment is a cheer to move on. Until finally what was once impossible is now accomplished.

As Zen master Jesus said, "If you have faith the size of a mustard seed… nothing will be impossible for you."

妥

妥

"Up from the

ashes

come the roses of success."

Ian Fleming

Chitty, Chitty Bang Bang

"Crash and burn."

It's a phrase that means to fail spectacularly. You don't just fail to achieve your goal, you end up worse off than where your started.

But at least you've started.

And if you should find yourselves covered in the ashes of your own spectacular failure; remember, ash makes excellent fertilizer.

Don't believe me?

Ask Walt Disney, Oprah Winfrey, Soichiro Honda, Vera Wang, Thomas Edison, Elvis Presley, Sidney Poitier, J.K. Rowling…

EVERY person who has achieved greatness in their field has dealt with failure, rejection, and ridicule. In short, they have been humbled.

Which is good, because when you are humbled, you turn to God for help.

As the disciple Peter says, "Humble yourselves therefore under the mighty hand of God, so that He may exalt you at the proper time."

So, when you are rejected, and your goals are ridiculed; give thanks knowing that help is on the way.

妥

妥

"The undoing is almost always more **difficult** than the doing."

Kate DiCamillo
The Magician's Elephant

There is a Zen parable about a student who seeks to learn sword fighting from a great master. He asks the master who long it will take. The master answers, "ten years." The student then pleads to learn faster and offers to work exceptionally hard. The master replies, "In that case, it will take thirty years."

Sometimes when we hurry, we make mistakes. Then we have to stop, fix the mistake, then start all over again. We end up taking twice as long as we would have if we had just taken our time and been mindful of what we were doing in the first place.

Fixing relationships can take even longer.

A careless word here, a raised voice there, can do damage that takes years to fix.

If it is good advice to think before you act; then it is better advice to think TWICE before you speak.

In every interaction, give respect to the object of your attention. See the divine in everyone and everything and treat them right the first time.

妥

妥

"ONE WORD
can sometimes be sharper
than a
THOUSAND SWORDS."

Mildred D. Taylor
Roll of Thunder,
Hear Me Cry

Just as a single word can sometimes bring enlightenment, a single word can sometimes bring devastation.

A word spoken in anger or derision can cause pain that lasts for years.

As Fa-kheu-pi-us notes, "To lightly laugh at and ridicule another is wrong."

And as Jesus said, "It is not what goes into the mouth that defiles a person, but it is what comes out of the mouth that defiles… for what comes out of the mouth proceeds from the heart."

So, the harsh words you speak to others are truly a measure of the harshness of your own heart.

The good news is that by monitoring your speech, you can effectively monitor your own spiritual growth. Are you expressing love for others with each word you speak? If so, you're on the right track. If not, think before you speak. Even when disagreeing, remember the divinity within the person before you and consider how your words may assist them on their journey.

Always remember to make your words sweet; in case you have to eat them later!

妥

妥

"Ain't 'cha gonna run?" she asked.
"No," he said, shoving the sheet away. "I'm gonna *fly.*"

Katherine Paterson
Bridge to Terabithia

Why walk when you can fly?

But humans can't fly!

But are we humans with a soul; or are we spirit beings having a human experience?

Both Jesus and the Buddha are reported to have walked on water. Both are reported to have walked through solid walls.

St. Joseph of Cupertino is reported to have actually levitated off the ground many times while saying mass. Numerous Buddhist monks have been reported levitating as well.

But that's not possible for humans!

And flying isn't possible for caterpillars. But the truth is, caterpillars and butterflies are the same thing. The butterfly just has a greater awareness of its true nature.

But before it could become a butterfly, it had to cocoon itself apart from the outside world, and turn within.

Maybe if we cocoon ourselves away in solitary meditation more often, we might discover the miracle of our own true nature. Then who knows what miracles we can accomplish!

妥

妥

"Field trips,

EVERYTHING

can change."

Tom Angleberger

Emperor Pickletine

Rides the Bus

Sometimes just changing your perspective can change your whole world. Whether seeing new things or seeing things in a new way, breaking up routines keeps us from falling into a rut, from becoming blinded by our own habits.

As Yogi Berra said, "When you come to the fork in the road, take it." It really doesn't matter which way you go, it only matters that you go.

Or in the words of the Taoist proverb, "The journey is the reward."

When we leave this life, we will not be able to take our accumulated wealth with us. If our soul carries anything with it at all, it will be the memories of our experiences. So, our experiences are indeed our treasures and our reward. And if we're open to it, our experiences might even change us for the better.

After all; what is life, but a field trip to this strange and wonderful place we call earth. Get out there and experience as much as you can!

妥

妥

"I've got the key to my

castle in the air,

but whether I can
unlock the door
remains to be seen."

Louisa May Alcott
Little Women

Indeed, our castle is "in the air" and not of this world. Consequently, many who turn to religion in the hopes of achieving greater worldly success are often disappointed.

Although spiritual enlightenment may bring us comfort in this world, its true goal is to prepare us for the next. That is where our castle awaits. To help us find our way home, the Buddha gave us four Noble Truths:

1. Life is full of suffering.
2. Suffering is caused by our attachments.
3. To overcome suffering, let go of attachments.
4. To let go of attachments, follow the Path (the Tao or the Way) of righteousness.

And Jesus gave us two simple commandments:

1. Love the Lord your God with all your heart and with all your soul and all your strength.
2. Love your neighbor as yourself. (Which also implies that we must love ourselves.)

These are the keys to our "castle in the air." They're as simple as a line from a children's book, yet more profound than volumes of philosophy – if you have the courage to use them.

妥

妥

You may have previously heard some of the insights contained in these pages; however, the point isn't to reveal new truths, but to remind you that the truths you seek are the truths you already know. If you can learn to live in a state of awareness, you can be reminded of these truths in the books you read, in the songs you hear, in your conversations with others, in the changing of the seasons…

Indeed, when the student is ready, the teacher will appear.

The reason that saying is true, is because EVERYTHING is a teacher - if you're able to learn from it.

So now it's your turn.

I've included a few bonus quotes for you. See what lessons they can teach you in the pages that follow…

妥

妥

"It is a goodly life that you lead, friend; no doubt the best in the world, if only you are

strong enough

to lead it!"

Kenneth Grahame

The Wind in the Willows

妥

妥

"All the
COLORS i AM
iNSiDE
have not been invented
yet."

Shel Silverstein

Where the Sidewalk Ends

妥

妥

"There should be a
place where
only the things you want
to happen, happen"

Maurice Sendak

Where the Wild Things Are

妥

妥

"If things start happening,
don't worry, don't stew,
just go right along and

**you'll start
happening too."**

‿◊‿

Dr. Seuss
Oh, The Places You'll Go

☯

妥

妥

"A heart is not judged by how much you

love;

but by how much you are

loved by others"

L. Frank Baum

The Wonderful

Wizard of Oz

妥

妥

"I have never tried that before, so I think I should **definitely be able** to do that."

Astrid Lindgren

Pippi Longstocking

妥

妤

"The same substance composes us - the tree overhead, the stone beneath us, the bird, the beast, the star -

WE ARE ALL ONE,

all moving to the same end."

P. L. Travers

Mary Poppins

妥

妥

Recommended Further Reading

Borg, Marcus. Jesus and Buddha: The Parallel Sayings. Berkeley: Ulysses Press, 1997.

Chung, Tsai Chih. Zen Speaks: Shouts of Nothingness. New York: Anchor Books, 1994.

Eliot, Sir Charles & Bowden, E. M. Revered Wisdom: Buddhism. New York: Sterling Innovation 2010.

Freke, Timothy. The Zen Koan Card Pack. New York: Stewart Tabori & Chang, 1997.

Hanh, Thich Nhat. Going Home: Jesus and Buddha as Brothers. New York: Riverhead Books, 1999.

Hoff, Benjamin. The Tao of Pooh. New York: Penguin Books, 1982.

Mascetti, Manuela Dunn & Barrett, Timothy Hugh (Editors.) The Little Book of Zen. New York: Barnes & Noble Books 2001.

妥

妥

About the author:

Brian Rock is a spiritual being currently having a human experience as a children's writer.

Brian's picture books

WHICH ANIMAL IS FASTEST?

MARTIAN MUSTACHE MISCHIEF

HAVE YOU SEEN JESUS?

THE DEDUCTIVE DETECTIVE

WITH ALL MY HEART

PIGGIES

DON'T PLAY WITH YOUR FOOD!

Brian's Chapter books:

THE TYLER FILES #1 Smarty Pants!

THE TYLER FILES #2 Hollow Weenie!

THE TYLER FILES #3 My Nose is Running!

Follow him on Twitter @BrianRockWrites

妥

妥

妥

妥

www.ingramcontent.com/pod-product-compliance
Lightning Source LLC
Chambersburg PA
CBHW021955090426
42811CB00001B/38